WITNESS
TO THE
COVENANT OF
CIRCUMCISION

WITNESS
TO THE
COVENANT OF
CIRCUMCISION

BRIS MILAH

DALE LIEBERMAN

𝒥𝒜

JASON ARONSON INC.
NORTHVALE, NEW JERSEY
LONDON

To Brooke and Boyce

♥ Dale

This book was set in 11 pt. Goudy by FASTpages of Nanuet, NY.

10 9 8 7 6 5 4 3 2 1

Library of Congress Cataloging-in-Publication Data

Lieberman, Dale.
    Witness to the covenant of circumcision : bris milah /
by Dale Lieberman.
        p.   cm.
    ISBN 1–56821–994–6 (alk. paper)
    1. Berit milah—Pictorial works.   I. Title.
BM705.L54   1997
296.4'422—dc21   96–48368

Manufactured in the United States of America. Jason Aronson Inc. offers books and cassettes. For information and catalog write to Jason Aronson Inc., 230 Livingston Street, Northvale, New Jersey 07647.

Dedicated
to the memory of
Sophie Ivker Lourie
Eshes Chayil
and
model of commitment
to the Jewish community

Contents

PREFACE

Jewish circumcision, *bris milah*, may be the oldest, continually practiced religious ritual in human civilization. Circumcision's ancient roots and its tenacious hold upon Jewish identity may be responsible for the ritual's surviving not only the persecutions of Jews throughout the ages but also the various assimilations of Jews in every society in which they have sojourned. Notwithstanding the importance of circumcision to the Jewish people, as commandment and as the tangible sign and performance of the covenant between God and the Jewish people, the ritual of *bris milah* has been and remains one of the most private and least visible forms of Jewish worship.

Since the Torah does not explain why it is circumcision that is commanded as the sign of the divine covenant with Jews, commentators have derived many "reasons", "justifications", and "explanations" for circumcision—among them: the control of lust and concupiscence, the domination of man's evil impulses by his more spiritual nature, the effectiveness of circumcision as a sign binding and identifying a people sharing a belief in the unity of God, and the perpetual symbolism of man's ability to perfect himself. Whatever the most attractive rationale, rationalization, or theory, circumcision has been historically associated with Jewish worship since the time of Abraham.

Recognizing that circumcision is not unique to the Jews but is a common practice in many societies, anthropologists have claimed to understand circumcision in a variety of ways—as a fertility ritual, as a means of clarifying descent, and as an initiation ritual separating a newborn male from his maternal caretakers and bringing him into the community of males. Other theories abound. Modern medicine has largely determined that circumcision has significant medical value as well, and circumcision has become a common secular practice.

The principal beneficiary of circumcision medically and religiously is the child himself. (Indeed, for the Jewish male the *bris* has been considered a prerequisite to full participation in the world-to-come, and the Jewish father who fails to provide for his son's circumcision would be considered derelict.) The suites of photographs contained in this volume reveal that there are additional beneficiaries at a *bris*, and it is their experience, as participants, worshippers, observers , and photographer, which is the primary subject of this documentary.

—Dale Lieberman

"And He said, 'Take your son . . . whom you love . . . .' "

BRIS IN NOVEMBER—SUITE ONE

November—Photograph One

Abraham received God's commandment to circumcise himself and every male of his family throughout the generations, as part of the covenant between them, and it is, accordingly, the Jewish father who is primarily obligated to have his son circumcised. However, the female members of the family customarily have original jurisdiction of the infant and surrender him as the first step of the *bris*.

Just as in biblical times animals to be sacrificed were to remain with their dam for seven days, a child to be circumcised may be considered to have dwelled with and been nurtured by his mother for seven days and must be given up and presented for the *bris* on the eighth day after his birth.

Joy and anxiety coexist in these moments, as the child is delivered in princely fashion through the community, which welcomes him with the greeting: "*Baruch Ha-Ba!* Blessed is the one who comes. Blessed is the one who comes to be circumcised on the eighth day!"

November—Photograph Two

The "older generation" takes great pleasure in shepherding one of the newest members of the community to his place on the *bimah*.

As this infant is to be initiated in the "Covenant of Abraham", he is both a symbol of God's promise to Abraham that his line would be fruitful and multiply and proof of the ongoing fulfillment of their covenant.

November—Photograph Three

Many synagogues have a special "Chair of Elijah", upon which a child to be circumcised is placed by an honored participant prior to delivery to the *sandek*. In homes, too, a chair is customarily designated and set aside for this purpose.

According to the rabbis, God granted the prophet Elijah the privilege of attending every *bris*. Elijah is also expected at every Passover *seder*, as the herald of the Messiah and the world-to-come.

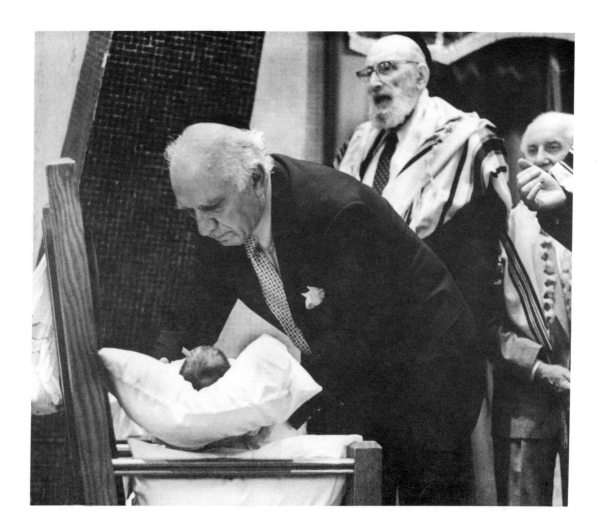

November—Photograph Four

A *bris* is a communal, religious occasion, and attendance is itself a *mitzvah*. The *bris* affords the opportunity for education, communication, thanksgiving, and celebration. Here, the father of the child delivers remarks he has prepared for the ceremony.

November—Photograph Five

Before proceeding with the circumcision, the *mohel* holds up the child for all to see. So too do Jews at the *shabbos* table traditionally raise and identify whole loaves of bread before blessing God.

November—Photograph Six

Here, the *mohel* lays the child on the pillow which the *sandek* will lower to his lap.

Serving as *sandek* is considered to be the greatest honor at a *bris*, for the *sandek*'s lap (upon which the *bris* is traditionally performed) is compared to the altar of atonement in the destroyed Temple, and the circumcision itself is likened to the burning of incense.

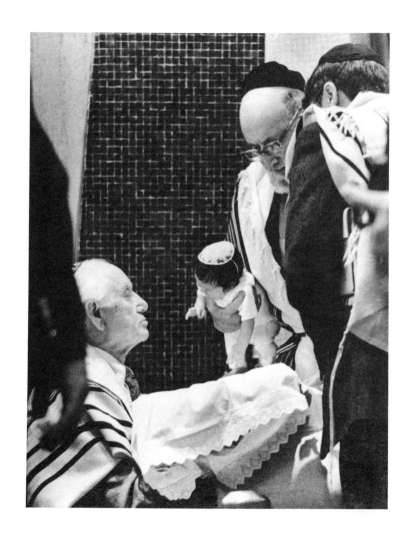

November—Photograph Seven

It is the father's obligation to cause his son to be circumcised. The Vilna Gaon (b. 1720) explained that the father is supposed to stand next to the *mohel* to appoint him as his agent (*Shulchan Aruch, Yoreh Deah 265*) because circumcision is like a sacrifice offered in the Temple of Jerusalem, where the offerer of a sacrifice would stand next to the priest and appoint him as his agent.

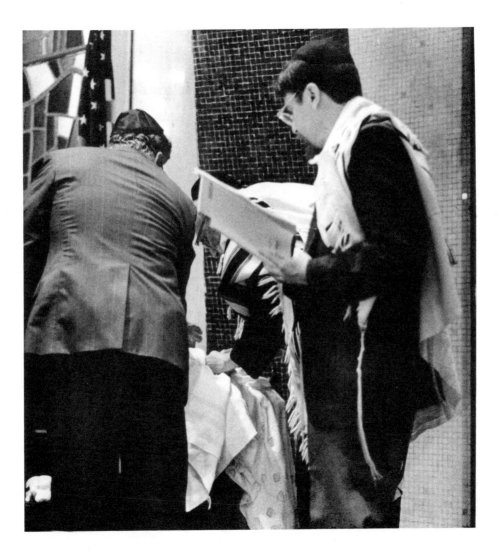

November—Photograph Eight

Here, after the surgery has been completed, the baby's sisters watch as the blessings over the wine are recited and the baby is given his name.

November—Photograph Nine

After the *bris* the *mohel*, retaining custody of the infant, gives instructions to the mother regarding subsequent care. Focused on her baby, from whom she has been separated throughout the *bris*, she reaches out for him.

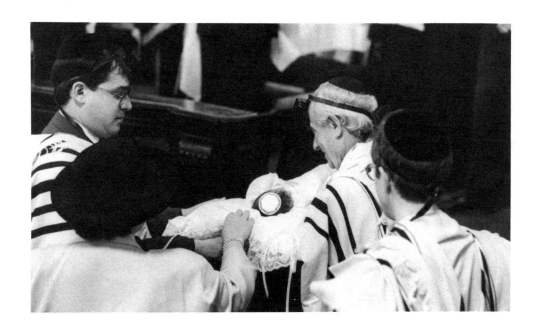

"	. . . [S]even days it shall be with its dam;
on the eighth day you shall give it to me."

BRIS IN APRIL—SUITE TWO

April—Photograph One

The morning prayers have just concluded. The principal male characters in the *bris milah* ritual are waiting for the drama of the ritual to unfold. They continue to wear their *talesim* [prayer shawls], and some, following a custom, will continue to wear their *t'fillin* [phylacteries] for the *bris*.

At the moment of this photograph the figures happen to be positioned according to the levels of holiness they represent in the drama:

In the foreground are the infant's father with his brother and father-in-law who are to participate in the delivery of the child to the *mohel*. Above and to the right is the rabbi (with a congregant). At the highest level, under the design of flames reaching to heaven on the curtain of the ark containing the Scrolls of Torah, are the *mohel*, his son (also a practicing *mohel*), and the child's paternal grandfather, who is to be the *sandek*.

April—Photograph Two

As in the Jewish priesthood of old, and in many a trade and profession, a son learns from and assists his father. Here, the *mohel's* son, already a certified *mohel* himself, assists his father in preparation for the *bris*, tying the fringes of the prayer shawl behind his father's back so that they do not interfere during the *bris*.

April—Photograph Three

*B*aruch Ha-Ba! Blessed is the one who comes. Blessed is the one who comes to be circumcised on the eighth day!

Cradled in an elaborate white pillow, the infant is brought down an aisle, like a bridegroom, through the section of the synagogue reserved for men. He is carried by his maternal aunt, with his mother close behind.

The child of the *bris* is referred to as the *chatan damim*, the "bridegroom of the blood" [of circumcision]. The next time he will come down the aisle as a ritual honoree may be as the bridegroom at his wedding, when he will also be referred to as a *chatan*.

April—Photograph Four

The males have taken possession of the child, upon whom eyes and care are focused. This child happens to be the first fruit of his mother and he is being consigned by another of his maternal aunts to the custody of his male relatives. As the father shall verbally authorize the *mohel* to perform the circumcision on his behalf, this surrender of the child by the women constitutes their consent, their authorization, and their participation in the *bris*.

> "The first-born of thy sons shalt thou give unto Me; . . . seven days it shall be with its dam; on the eighth day thou shalt give it to Me." (Exodus 22:29)

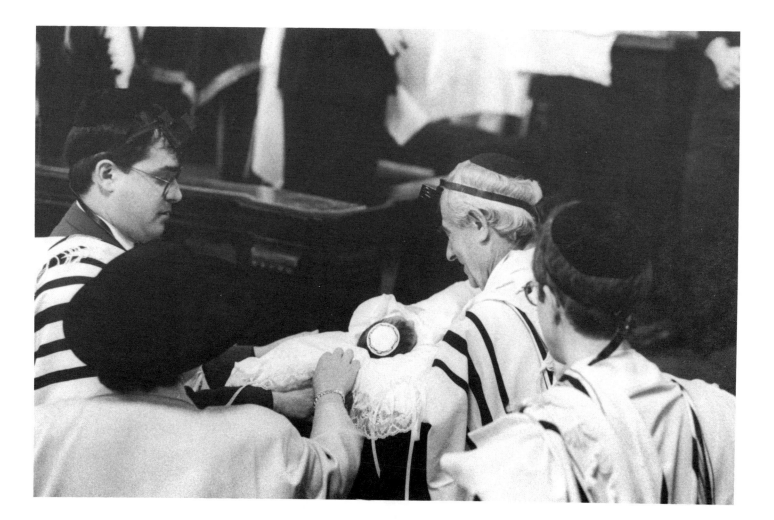

April—Photograph Five

A person appointed to participate in the delivery of the child for circumcision not only receives a public honor and a share in the performance of a *mitzvah*, but also serves as a subscriber and witness to the ratification and fulfillment of a holy covenant. Here the person so honored conveys the child to the father who has been waiting on the *bimah* with the *sandek* and *mohel*.

April—Photograph Six

The *sandek*, here the paternal grandfather, naturally radiant, receives spiritual benefit from his honor. The circumcision on his lap, like a sacrifice upon an altar, has served to atone for his sins, and by virtue of his service he has been purified.

April—Photograph Seven

The anthropologists of religion speak of rites of initiation as symbolic death and rebirth. Here, the cutting of flesh and the drawing of blood, though short of death, elicits an emotion short of mourning. The rabbi comforts the father as the commandment is performed. Here, with God's name Shaddai written on his hand by the straps of his *t'fillin* (*Shin-Dalet-Yod*), it is as if Shaddai himself were delivering reassurance and comfort.

April—Photograph Eight

The child, although fully a person before, is symbolically reborn at the *bris*. As the rabbi gives the child his name, he quotes from the Book of Ezekiel (16:6) saying, with cup of wine in hand, "And I passed by you and saw you down-trodden in your blood, and I said to you, 'In your blood, live!' and I said to you, 'In your blood, live!' ". Drops of wine are given to the child, recalling God's gift of life and prosperity to the people Israel.

April—Photograph Nine

Once the public drama of the *bris* has been completed, the infant's extravagant pillow is replaced by a desktop. The child, no longer the object of the covenant ritual and the vehicle of communal intensification and salvation, has become a baby whose post-surgical care needs to be explained by the *mohel*. The drama is over, and the child needs to be re-integrated into the world as a subject. This is the transition.

April—Photograph Ten

The paternal grandfather, sometime *sandek*, has been renewed and can again nourish the younger generation. His liquor flows. *L'chaim!*

April—Photograph Eleven

Within this circle of life from one generation to the next, the child's uncle leads the customary blessings after a meal, the *bensching*—expanded at the festive meal following a *bris* to include special blessings for the parents and child.

"Circumcision . . . is a very, very hard thing. . . ."

BRIS IN DECEMBER—SUITE THREE

December—Photograph One

Hanukkah. 8:30 a.m. The customary morning prayers have already been recited in this basement sanctuary of an old synagogue, whose main sanctuary is not easily heated in winter. Taking advantage of the educational opportunity afforded by this gathering for the *bris*, the child's father (himself a rabbi) explains the history and significance of *bris milah*.

December—Photograph Two

The child's mother has given up her baby to the godmother who will in turn deliver him to the men for the *bris*.

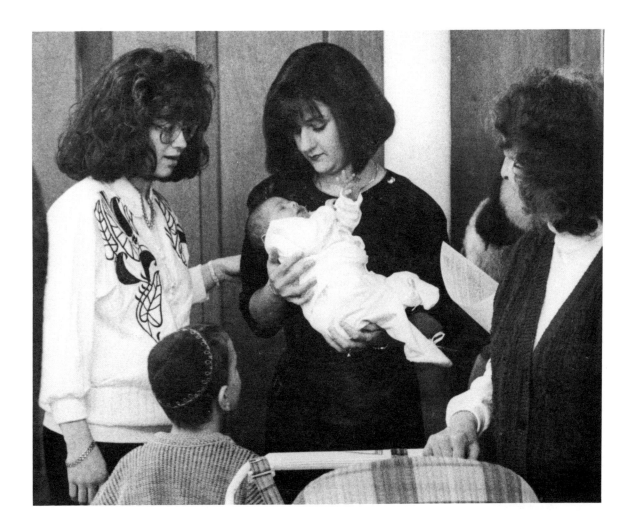

December—Photograph Three

As the *kvatterin* (godmother), dressed in black, delivers the child to the white-hooded *kvatter* (godfather), the child makes the symbolic transition from impurity to purity, from the profane to the sacred, from the birth process to ritual worship.

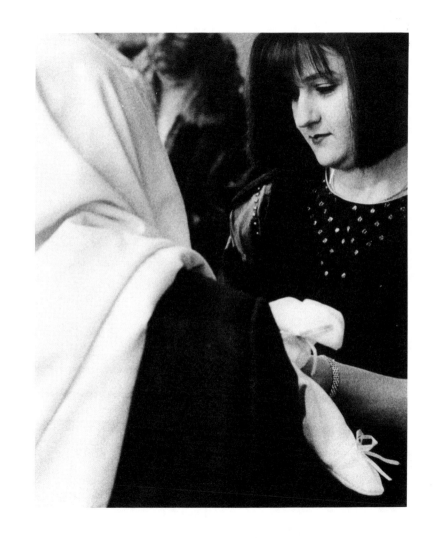

December—Photograph Four

During the initial progress from the women to the men to the place of circumcision, the participants focus on the humanity and personality of the infant, with all the tenderness one associates with the nurturing of newborn infants.

December—Photograph Five

As the child is brought closer to the place of circumcision, as the holiness of space and time intensifies, the child seems to become more object than subject. The *kvatter*, as well as the father, caught up in the prayer of the ritual, seem to distance themselves from the personality of the child.

December—Photograph Six

The selection of a *mohel* is very important to many parents in many communities. As well as for technical competency, he is often chosen for his good character and observance of all the laws of Judaism. During the *bris* the *mohel* is at once agent of the father, representative of the community, and priest of God. His role is awesome.

December—Photograph Seven

"Circumcision is a very, very hard thing," wrote Maimonides, the great 12th century philosopher—an act to be performed promptly, when it is easier for the parents, before the imaginative form compelling them to love the child consolidates.

December—Photograph Eight

For many Jews the naming of the child during the blessings upon the wine is the most meaningful part of the *bris milah* ceremony. Those for whom or in whose memory he is named are honored at the same time he is given his Jewish identity. At this time the child has fully entered the covenantal community.

December—Photograph Nine

After the *bris* had been completed and while the festive meal was underway, this woman—who had served as godmother—was noticed at prayer, alone. This accidental photograph witnessed and memorialized her prayer. The honor given to this woman was considerate and deliberate. A childless woman hoping for a child may be selected to serve as *kvatterin* to increase the likelihood that her prayers for a child will be answered. The *bris* of her son, less than ten months later, is the subject of the following suite of photographs.

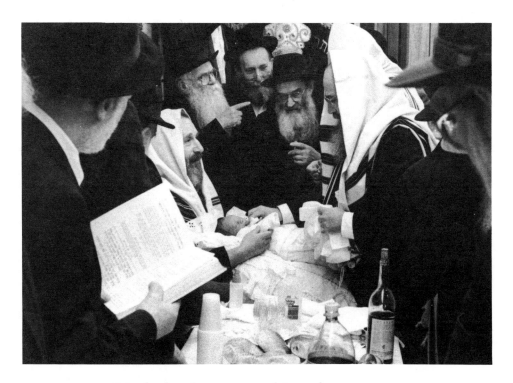

*"As he has been entered into the covenant,
so may he be introduced to Torah, the chuppah,
and the performance of good deeds"*

BRIS IN OCTOBER—SUITE FOUR

October—Photograph One

Well before the *minyan* has formed for the morning prayers, tables are laid for the *seudat mitzvah*, the meal planned to follow and celebrate the *bris*. Here, preparations for serving this meal are begun by young and old. Soon a curtain will be dropped to create separate space for the women—for the prayers and for the ritual of the *bris milah* itself.

October—Photograph Two

A portion from the Torah is read publicly during the weekday morning service on Mondays and Thursdays. On this day the maternal grandfather and father of the infant have been given *aliyot*, the honor of going up to the Torah, for portions of the reading.

October—Photograph Three

The *mohel* has an audience, even for his preparations, as he readies his instruments for the *bris*.

October—Photograph Four

The infant, cushioned securely upon the elaborate pillow prepared for the occasion, is here passed from the women to the men as the ritual order commences at 10:00 a.m.

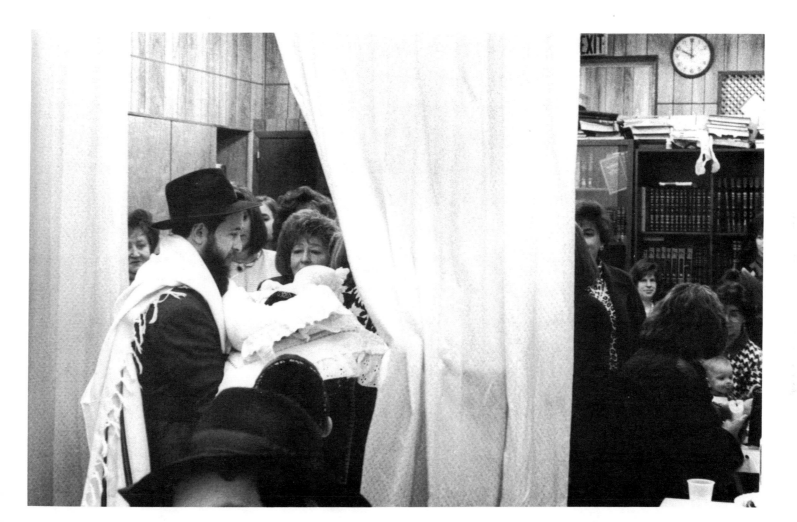

October—Photograph Five

As the *mohel* lays the child on the lap of the *sandek*, the father (at the right) recites a personal prayer—appointing the *mohel* as his agent, asking that the commandment be considered like a delightful fragrance, and praying for blessings to reward the presentation of his first fruits as fulfillment of the commandment.

October—Photograph Six

The new male member increases and refreshes the community. The principal adult participants in the ritual have continued to wear their prayer shawls after the morning service. Their doing so not only includes the *bris* in their personal morning worship, but also emphasizes their role as community representatives as they sanctify an ancient ritual.

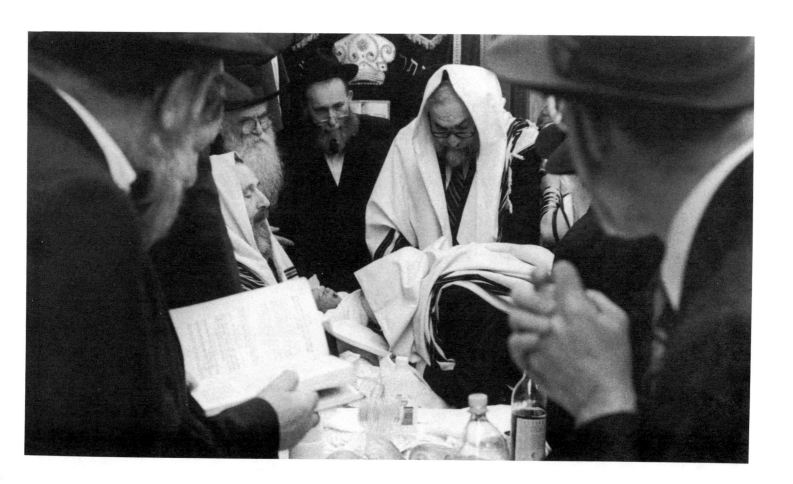

October—Photograph Seven

The baby celebrates his first *kiddush* as a new initiate in Jewish civilization as he receives drops of wine taken by the *mohel* from the cup of blessing. He has joined, body and blood, the community of men around him. They have been fruitful; they have multiplied. As he is refreshed, they are refreshed.

October—Photograph Eight

As Hannah was witnessed in prayer by the priest Eli, who asked God to grant whatever prayer she had made (for a child, as related in the first book of Samuel), so in prayer the mother of the infant at this *bris* had been witnessed by this unwitting photograph—taken less than ten months earlier, when she had been the *kvatterin* at the *bris* which is the subject of the preceding suite of photographs. The new mother gratefully holds the portrait of her, with an inscription relating her prayers to Hannah's.

"This is my covenant which you shall keep between me and your children and your descendants; you shall circumcise every male born to you. . . . "

BRIS IN MAY—SUITE FIVE

May—Photograph One

Prerequisite to fulfilling the covenant, a sacred space must
be created, and here in the home of a couple married but
two years, the nearly vacant dining room will be chosen by
the *mohel*, upon his arrival, for its space and for its light.

May—Photograph Two

The space is consecrated by the construction of an "altar" made of wood (an alternative to the lap of the *sandek*). The *mohel* has found in the corner an old sewing table, which he unfolds with the assistance of the father and grandfather of the child to be circumcised.

May—Photograph Three

This *mohel*, also a pediatrician, administers a local lidocaine anesthetic prior to commencing the ceremony. The child's cry of pain resulting from the injection elicits the outreach of his grandfather.

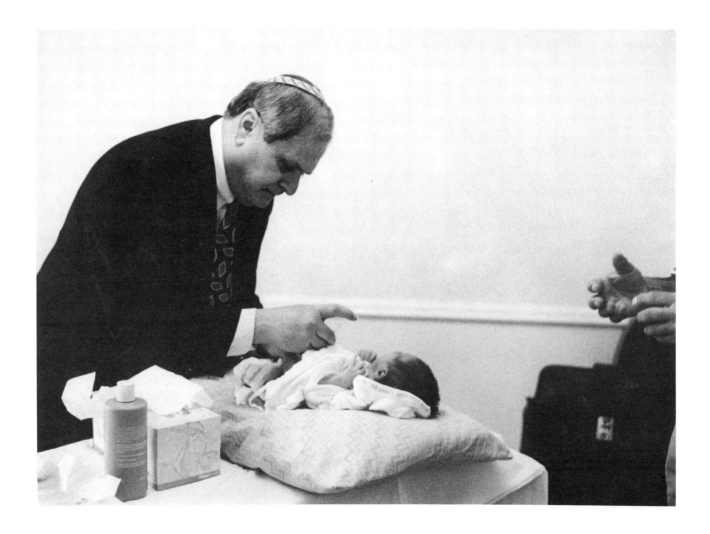

May—Photograph Four

The *mohel* explains to the family the ritual of *bris milah*. *Mohalim* often assume the role of educator at these ceremonies, which are precious opportunities for Jewish education.

May—Photograph Five

The mother's sensibility, expressed in this photograph, is common to many who are drawn to watch the physical reality of circumcision. Traditionally, the mother of the infant to be circumcised stays at a distance from the scene, for a variety of reasons—psychological, social, religious, and anthropological.

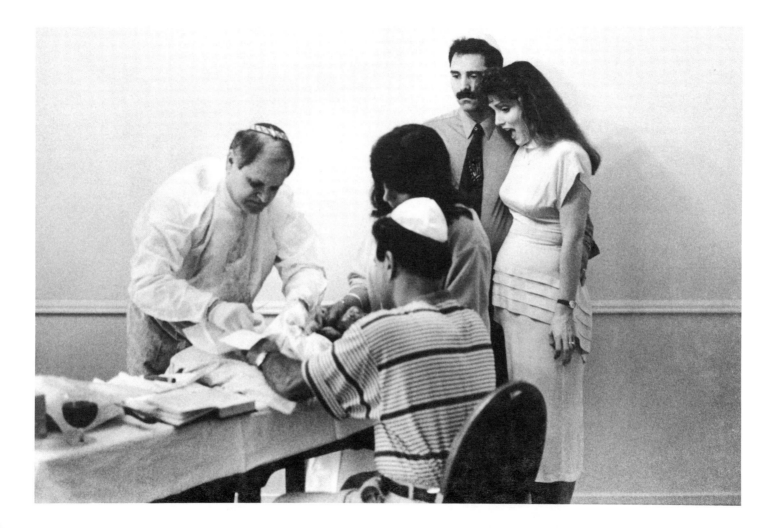

May—Photograph Six

The family members derive comfort from each other at a time that is often more difficult for the parents than it is for the infant.

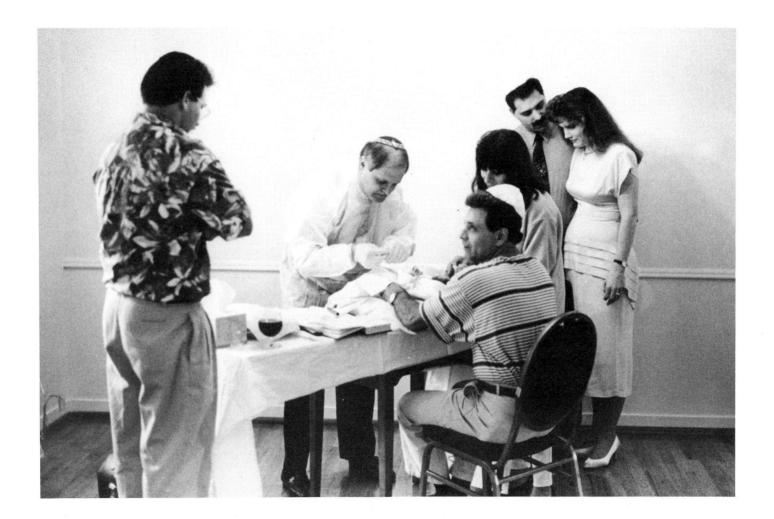

May—Photograph Seven

Drawing a small amount of blood from the wound (*metz-itzah*) was recognized as a requirement in the Talmud and is considered an essential part of the *bris milah* ritual.

May—Photograph Eight

However painless circumcision may be, due to the speed of the *mohel*, the local anesthesia, or the immaturity of nerve endings in the extra skin, the minor surgery of circumcision becomes, as a result of the ritual process and its organization of time and space, an event producing anxiety and stress—relieved only by its conclusion.

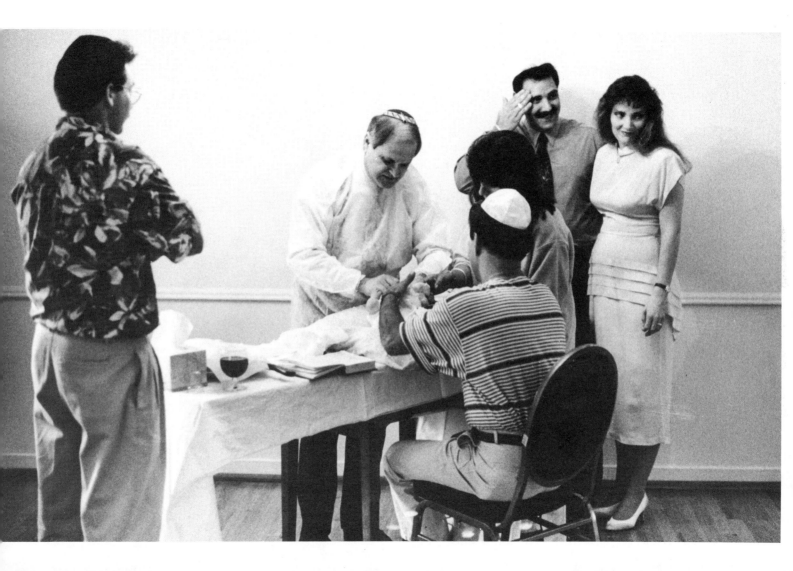

May—Photograph Nine

The *mohel* had asked, at the outset, that *challah* for blessing be placed and covered on the table of circumcision. At the conclusion of the *bris*, the grandfather says the traditional blessing for bringing forth bread from the earth, cuts the loaf, and symbolically begins the obligatory festive meal.

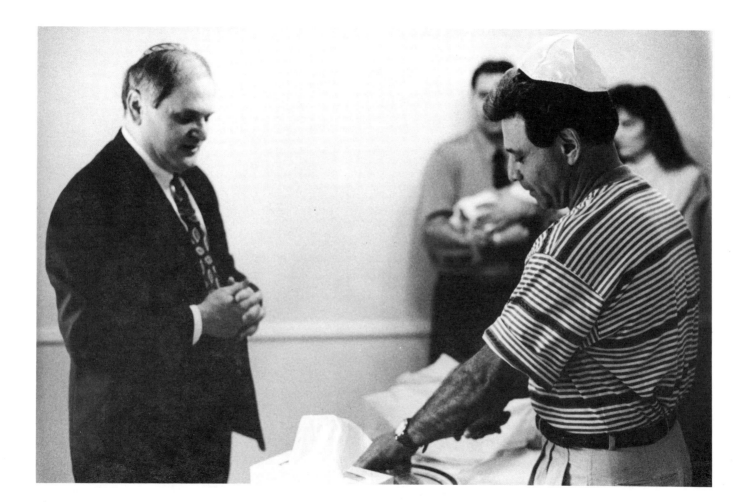

May—Photograph Ten

Relieved and satisfied after his commitment to Jewish tradition has been tried and tested, the father cradles his child and cools off.

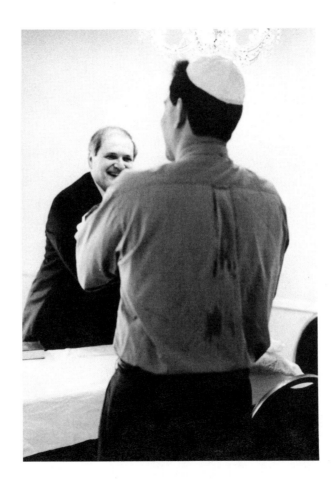

"Sustain this child for his father and mother" and
may they *"rejoice in their offspring."*

AFTERWORD

The commandment of *bris milah* sets up a drama to be played out at a sacred time, eight days after the birth of a Jewish male, in a sacred place, selected or created. The principal characters, the family, are naturally selected, the *mohel* engaged, and the community of fellow worshippers, friends, and neighbors welcomed. The drama orchestrates a progression of feelings, from joy to awe, to pain, to atonement, expiation, relief, satisfaction, and celebration. The drama is repeated from one *bris* to the next, organizing the emotions, as well as space and time. The ritual of *bris milah* not only initiates the child but also re-initiates the other participants into the covenantal community of Jewish progenitors. As the sign of the covenant is imposed, Jewish commitment is tested and forged.

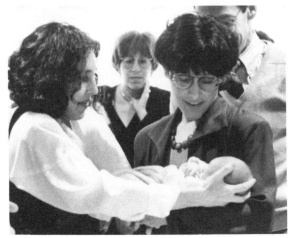

About the Author

Dale Lieberman is a photographer and lawyer in Philadelphia, Pennsylvania. He is a graduate of Yale College, where he majored in Religious Studies, and the University of Pennsylvania Law School, where he served on the *Law Review*. Mr. Lieberman has discovered in documentary photography the opportunity to communicate the phenomenon of subjective religious experience. He is the author of the essay "Bris Milah" which appeared in the Winter, 1994, issue of *Kerem*. Mr. Lieberman resides with his wife, Jane Porcelan, and their three children, Sarah, David, and Daniel.